Virginia

Quilting Cancer
Seeking solace while quilting blocks and fighting cancer

Kelly Fanning

and

Erin Fanning, Contributing Editor

Copyright © 2017 Erin Fanning

All rights reserved.

ISBN-10: 197618357X
ISBN-13: 978-1976183577

DEDICATION

For all courageous people and the legacies they leave behind.

CONTENTS

	Acknowledgments and a Quilted Cover	
	Preface: The Fiber of Humanity	1
	Part 1: Quilting Cancer	3
1	About Kelly and Quilting Cancer	4
2	I Found Inspiration—and Quilting—As I Was Dying	5
3	Oh, the Mamas I Have Known!	8
4	God, Goats, and His Good Grace	11
5	Choosing Smiles Over Tears	15
6	Me and My Co-Stars	19
7	Pollyanna and Her Pity Party	23
8	My Daughter is a Grappler	26
9	The All-True Adventures of Kelly on Chemo	29
10	Bald is Beautiful	32
11	It's Complicated	36
12	A Loving Tribute to a Source of Inspiration	39
13	Guilt is My Frequent Companion…	42
	Part 2: A Sister's Journal	46
1	Pig Whisperer	47

2	A Timeless Life	50
3	Reading in Tandem	53
4	The World Stopped	56
5	Grace Notes	58
6	Ride In Peace	63
	About the Authors	64

ACKNOWLEDGEMENTS AND A QUILTED COVER

Kelly made the three quilts decorating the cover of this book for her daughters Shaelyn, Sierra, and Sheridan. She carefully crafted them, laying out each pattern and then stitching the pieces together. Soon more quilts were planned, a never-ending list of projects for the people she loved, reflecting a grateful heart.

I understood her desire, wanting to thread all that love together into a continuous patchwork of selflessness and generosity. And so, in my own small way, I made an attempt to recognize the countless people who helped Kelly and my family during her battle with cancer. The result was *Grace Notes*, an essay you can find on page 58.

Today, I imagine those same people continuing to spread their love, cloaking kindness and encouragement around the shoulders of others who struggle with adversity, connecting us all together in an endless quilt of humanity, which is exactly what Kelly would have wanted.

~Erin Fanning

PREFACE: THE FIBER OF HUMANITY

"I don't want you think I'm unhappy," my sister Kelly told me during the fall of 2016. "I'm really quite happy."

She spoke from her bed, brain metastases having left her partially paralyzed on her right side. A physical therapist had departed moments earlier, and, combined with radiation treatment from the previous day, Kelly was exhausted.

As I sat there, chattering about this and that, trying to take her mind off her circumstances, I wondered what emotion my face had betrayed to make Kelly want to reassure me. Even more importantly, what invisible strength allowed her to find happiness at that moment, during the most difficult time of her life?

None of us know how we will react when faced with life-threatening challenges until they hit us. We can only hope to have the courage and optimism that Kelly possessed, continuing to approach life with dignity and enthusiasm while taking on new interests and maintaining a genuine concern for others.

Sometimes we become witnesses to these acts of bravery, only somewhat aware at the time, but later able to appreciate the full magnitude of what we experienced. During the aftermath, there is a sense, almost an obligation, of wanting to share these everyday stories of inspiration with a larger audience.

I know I'm not alone. Many of us brush shoulders with unforgettable acts of courage, people who possess an unlimited well of resilience. They will themselves forward, accepting their circumstances yet never giving up.

Their stories are often quiet, unfolding without fanfare, but they encompass the fiber of humanity, a silent strength that weaves us all together. And the more we know about these people, the stronger we become as a society.

So I've chosen to record Kelly's journey with adversity, her eight-year battle with cancer. My intention is not to turn her into a saint or deify her. Like all of us, Kelly had faults, yet at the end of her life, she revealed a core strength and selflessness. She learned how to fully live while also preparing to die.

She shared her battle through Quilting Cancer, a blog she started while teaching herself how to quilt, which is reproduced here in Part One. Part Two includes my observations and the lessons Kelly taught me.

Her message transcends time and location. It is the universal call to embrace life despite one's circumstances. It speaks of compassion—Kelly was constantly aware of others' needs, always thankful for even the smallest assistance—and finding joy in the simplest everyday occurrences.

To borrow from Proverbs 3:3—a verse I return to again and again—Kelly's lessons will never leave me. They are bound around my neck, written on the tablet of my heart. ~Erin

PART 1 QUILTING CANCER

1. ABOUT KELLY AND QUILTING CANCER

I was diagnosed with a rare and incurable cancer eight years ago. With my diagnosis, I learned the depth of fear, the paralysis of anxiety, and the fragility of hope. I have had four surgeries, radiation, six chemotherapy protocols, and participated in three clinical trials. Currently, I am receiving an experimental drug that will hopefully help my immune system to combat the cancer. And if not, I am hoping to be accepted into another clinical trial. Although I did not choose this journey with cancer, I have learned that I can choose the manner in which I ride it out.

I have learned to live in the moment, find adventure in each day, and turn toward the places where I find inspiration. Throughout all, I am raising my three daughters, managing my household (which includes horses, dogs, cats, chickens, and goats), and taking on new adventures. That's where the title of this blog, Quilting Cancer, comes from. Somewhere during the dark days of winter I decided I would create quilts for each of my daughters. Having never quilted before, as I submersed myself in patterns and colors and fabrics, I found adventure in what I was doing. With each stitch and each quilt, I found solace. And the idea for this blog was born.

I hope that you will follow my blog, find inspiration and joy, share comments—and perhaps some quilts. I would like to fill the photo gallery with pictures of quilts—yours and mine—and especially if the quilt was made by or belongs to someone whose life has been affected by cancer. Happy Quilting! ~Kelly~

2. I FOUND INSPIRATION—AND QUILTING—AS I WAS DYING

May 7, 2015

Last September I was dying. Literally dying. The cancer had taken over, treatment had failed, and I had run out of options. My body was also failing. As I struggled to breathe, even the smallest of daily activities zapped me of what little energy I had left. Hospice had come to my home, and I had become dependent on family and friends to run my household. I was hopeful that I would live to see my 50th birthday in October and have one last Christmas with my daughters. In fact, I had begun to prepare my family and friends, and most significantly, my three daughters, for the inevitable. I had resigned myself to the knowledge that it was unlikely I would live to see my eldest daughter turn 18 in January, let alone graduate from high school in May. And I came to terms with the knowledge that I would not see her sisters into adulthood.

As I filled hope chests for my girls with mementos and family heirlooms, gifts for future birthdays, graduations, and even weddings, I experienced a curious calm. I wrote in journals, finished photo albums, and reviewed my will for accuracy. I labeled specific items for each daughter, my sister, and friends. And through all of this, I found renewed purpose. Even a pleasant sense of accomplishment. Being someone who hates to leave the party early, I suppose I thought that I would at least leave on my own terms. But more than that, I recognized that these seemingly small accomplishments had given me something to look forward to and were even a source of inspiration.

And that brings me to the topic for today's post—inspiration and the places where we find it. Perhaps as I talk about inspiration, you will find that we are on common ground. In late September, a couple of significant things happened to me. First, I began to regularly meet with my friend and pastor, Mark. I asked him to help me prepare for death—I had specific questions and spiritual concerns (that I will address in a future blog posting titled "Fighting to Live While Preparing to Die"). These meetings have helped me to find inspiration in my relationship with God and in the knowledge that Christ is always with me. I have learned the power of prayer and am humbled to be the recipient of so many prayers all over the world.

And then the second thing happened… my beloved oncologist, Jonathan, suggested another chemotherapy treatment. As he explained, although it would not be without risks, I really had nothing to lose. But for the first time in more than seven years, I understood why cancer patients turn away from treatment. For the first time in more than seven years, I was too tired and too sick to continue. He gave me a few days to think it over, but I thought that I had made up my mind. Then soon after, a nurse called to check on me. I told her that Jonathan had suggested another chemo, and I could hear her typing on a computer. She let out a short laugh and said "Well he knows you, Kelly. You're already scheduled for Tuesday." After we hung up the phone I decided I might as well show up… and I've been showing up every Tuesday since then.

One day a short time later, I happened to be at my mother's house where she has an old quilt draped across the end of a bed. The quilt was made entirely by hand by my great, great, great aunt Mary Pfost in Idaho in the early 1900s. As I looked at that quilt, I considered the effort and creativity that had gone into its making and the pleasure it had brought to generations. She had left us with a beautiful legacy as well as an expression of herself. At that moment, although I had never quilted and really knew nothing about it, I decided I would create quilts for each of my daughters. It would be an adventure of sorts. I would learn a new skill, and my girls would have something that I had made specifically for each of them. I would pick designs and colors that would tell a story—the story of my love for them and of their personalities—and the quilts would be my legacy. Since then

I have, of course, learned the challenges as well as the pleasures of quilting. I have found solace in the stitches, been stimulated by the colors and fabrics, and comforted by the camaraderie of other quilters. I have finished one quilt, nearly finished another, and have two more in progress. This new adventure has inspired me.

As I prepare for my daughter's graduation next week, I consider every day since that first Tuesday, to be miraculous gifts. I'm not magically cured; I still require treatment; and I live with an uncertain future. I allow an occasional wallow in self-pity, and fear and anxiety still raise their ugly heads. But I also see beauty in each day and find something—some small adventure such as quilting—to look forward to. For now, cancer has been beat back, and I can reflect on what inspires me. For the next few weeks, I will write about inspiration and the five areas of my life where I find it… in my relationship with God, in my relationship with everyone else, in the mystery of motherhood, in the art of mindfulness, and in finding adventure every day.

I hope that you will join me and that you will share your thoughts and inspirations. I hope that something I say might spark inspiration for someone who needs it. Mostly, I think that you will find that we are on common ground, and that in itself is inspiring. ~Kelly~

3. OH, THE MAMAS I HAVE KNOWN!

May 10, 2015

Oh, the mamas I have known! They have been my role models and source of inspiration! Of course, my own tops this list, but this also includes my grandmothers, aunts, cousins, and friends. These amazing women have taught me so much about life, from how to drive a stick shift to the pleasure of a good book to the power of prayer. It was my grandmother, expert seamstress, who taught me to sew and bought me my first (and only) sewing machine. That Bernina dates back to 1980, and really my grandmother is largely responsible for the quilting I am doing now. I often think of her as I sit at the machine, foot on the pedal, fabric moving across the presser foot.

When I talk about inspiration and the five areas of my life where I find it, I normally discuss my relationship with God first. But in honor of Mother's Day, I have chosen to start with the Mystery of Motherhood. I don't think He will mind. He did, after all, in His great wisdom, create the mamas. And really, with this category of inspiration, I'm not just referring to mamas. I'm also referring to the daddies, grandparents, aunts and uncles, godparents, friends… anyone who is in a position to affect the response of a child. Anyone who is a role model for children. Including grown children. I simply refer to this category of inspiration as the Mystery of Motherhood because I am a mother (and because I like the title).

Several years ago, I attended the funeral of a friend who had died much too young of cancer. The priest that conducted the service talked about the many ways in which my friend knew God and God knew her. One of the ways that he listed was the "Mystery of Motherhood." I've never forgotten what he said, how he described the gift of motherhood and the role that we play in shaping our children. He spoke of my friend's legacy and how her courage and her presence would live on through her sons. And I appreciated that this priest recognized the significance of the gift of motherhood. So I've stolen the title from him, and if I knew his name I would give him credit now.

Not only do I have a great mom, but I was lucky enough to be born to great parents who were also born to great parents. They were amazing role models for my sister and me. They taught us and shaped us, gave us boundaries, knowing we would step over the lines, and loved us without condition. And they set examples for us that have been our blueprints for life and for our responses to the challenges that life has given us. They instilled in us a sense of adventure, a confidence that allowed us to risk, and a security that let us know we were never alone.

When I was a child, my father worked internationally. With a new country, there was much to learn… sometimes a new language, certainly a new social system. My parents learned to navigate this new place, find a home, place us in school, and take on cultural nuances. They faced these challenges (and I'm sure homesickness) with poise and pluck—at least that's how my childhood memory recalls it.

Later, when my father was in his 50s, he was diagnosed with cancer. His diagnosis and prognosis were grim. Yet my parents faced that crisis with courage and dignity and grace. I know that my father hurt, that he didn't feel well, that he was sad, and that he might have been afraid, yet, together with my mother, he set an example that I will never forget. And so as I face my own crisis, I try to do so with the same courage and grace and dignity that my parents modeled for me. Because, you see, it is my hope that my daughters will learn from my example. And someday, if they are faced with their own crisis, they will remember their mother and the example that I set. And they will face their own crisis with courage and grace and dignity.

And how do we do this? How do we face challenge and crisis with courage and grace and dignity? We pull from the memories that I have just described. We think of the parents, grandparents, aunts and uncles, friends, and mentors that have paved the way for us. And then we put one foot in front of the other, we pull ourselves up by the bootstraps, and we get back in the saddle. In the words of Winston Churchill, we "never, never, never give up."

So to all you courageous, graceful, dignified mamas, happy Mother's Day! ~Kelly~

4. GOD, GOATS, AND HIS GOOD GRACE

June 2, 2015

This morning while the air was cool, I lay in the hammock under our corkscrew willow tree, covered with a quilt, gently rocked by a breeze, looking up through the branches to the blue sky streaked with wispy white clouds. I contemplated the events of the day before. I had played midwife for our dairy goat, Mia. I was with her when she went in to labor, with her as she paced and her contractions increased, and with her as she delivered her twins. She had no idea when her pain would end. She grinded her teeth, she called out, she stoically pushed (never once asking for an epidural). Twin number one, a doeling, presented perfectly—front feet first followed by her head. Less than an hour later twin number two, a buckling, presented. But not perfectly. He was breech, his little bottom the first body part to come into the world. He didn't start breathing quite as easily as his sister had and suddenly stillness settled over the barn. Everything seemed to become very quiet and very slow. But Mia, appearing to ignore her physical discomfort, immediately set to work, nuzzling, licking, and stimulating the little guy to cough and sneeze and eventually to nurse. It was not the first time I would be in awe of the miracle of birth and of an animal's innate ability to care for her offspring.

Since the birth, I've been out to the barn about every two hours to check on Mia and her kids. They are staying warm, nursing well, and have gained their footing. And as I lay in the hammock this morning on my return trip from the barn, I contemplated God's creation, the beauty and grace of what I had witnessed, and the relative ease with which we accept life's events. My contemplation led me to think about the inspiration that I find in God. And that brings me to the second of my blog posts about inspiration (the first having been the Mystery of Motherhood).

Perhaps for the first time in my life, my diagnosis with cancer brought me face to face with the depth of fear and the crushing hold of anxiety. In the days following my diagnosis, there were so many unanswered questions. Had the cancer spread? Could it be treated? Cured? And perhaps most significantly to me, would I see my children grow up? Would I have an opportunity to see their stories unfold? I quickly learned that the answers to those questions were not simple and that cancer would, in many ways, control my life. As I learned to live within the confines of the ambiguity of cancer, I also learned that my fears, my runaway thoughts, my pounding heart could indeed be soothed by my relationship with God.

In my early days of cancer, I read an Anglican prayer that seemed to express what I was feeling. Too lengthy to memorize in my panicked state, I shortened it and edited it. That prayer became my mantra. As I lay on exam tables submitting myself to difficult, painful, and sometimes humiliating tests, I repeated the prayer to myself over and over. As I sat in exam rooms waiting for someone to relay the dreaded test results, I repeated the prayer. As I recovered from surgeries and treatment side effects, I repeated the prayer. And now as I wait to be accepted into yet another clinical trial, I repeat the prayer. With prayer, I have found that my mind stops racing, my heart slows down, and my anxiety becomes manageable. My prayer goes like this, "Heavenly Father, please wrap your arms around me and fill my heart with your love and your courage." I repeat it over and over. And I swear that there are times when I feel a gentle pressure across my shoulders.

As I describe the inspiration I find in God, my purpose here is not to prove the existence of God, nor is it to define the Holy Trinity or to tout an expertise in Scripture. My purpose is to merely explain the inspiration I find in my relationship with God—to illustrate the strength and courage I find in knowing that He is beside me through every step of this journey with cancer. That knowledge, demonstrated through Scripture and supported by faith and prayer, is the most consistent source of comfort that I have. In fact, I cannot imagine this journey without it. Because without my relationship with God, what possible point could there be in any of this? And what would there be to look forward to?

As a child, I dutifully memorized the Lord's Prayer, the books of the Old Testament and the New Testament, the Nicene Creed, the 23rd Psalm. I learned to genuflect, sporadically read my Bible, and I prayed. But really, and I'm ashamed to admit this, I believe that I took my relationship with God for granted. Looking back, I believe I was a fair-weather friend. I'm not so sure that I prayed whole heartedly. And I'm pretty sure that at times, I ignored what I knew God expected of me. I suppose I assumed that God would always be there for me and that I could come and go as I pleased. I have said that I feel a little hypocritical now because I rely on God when I once did not. But I also know that He has indeed always been there—and that I was fooling only myself—He was patiently waiting for me.

One of my favorite worship experiences was in Alaska. I lived in a remote area and an Episcopal priest would fly in once a month from Fairbanks. Our service was conducted in a borrowed church, I played the piano (generally any hymns that I pleased), and we always had a potluck dinner—caribou sausage, moose meat chili, and wild berry pie. Sometimes the weather was too severe for the priest to land his plane—yes, he was also the pilot. But generally, the entire congregation was present for every service. What I liked so much about that church experience is that because it was only once a month that we were all together to take communion, to sing, and to pray, we weren't likely to miss the service. We didn't take it for granted.

Early in my journey with cancer, a friend loaned me the book *The Shack* by William Paul Young. If you've not read it, I suggest you do. It's not generally my reading style—not the type of novel I gravitate toward. I won't spoil the story for you, but it contained an important take home message. WE ARE NEVER ALONE! Christ is always with us, and because he lived and suffered, he knows our suffering. He faced his own trial, humiliation, and crucifixion with dignity and courage and grace. Who could be more inspiring? So although I may have to continue putting one foot in front of the other through this journey, He walks it beside me, never leaving me.

I am aware that I am the recipient of prayers all over the world. As news of my diagnosis spread, as treatments worked and failed, as I have met new challenges, family and friends have prayed for me. And then they have told their family and friends to pray for me. People have come to my home, held my hands, placed their arms around my shoulders, and prayed for me. I have been added to prayer lists and masses. That is both humbling and strengthening. And just as I have felt the strength of prayer, I hope that others do as I pray for them.

And so, as I lay in the hammock, having played midwife to a goat and admiring the beauty that surrounds me, I find myself inspired by God, His creation, and His grace. ~Kelly~

5. CHOOSING SMILES OVER TEARS

June 18, 2015

(Note: This blog entry in an interruption of my five-part series on inspiration. With this entry, I will write about what it means, according to me, to be a survivor.)

The mood was festive—almost celebratory. It was early on a warm June evening, and we had gathered at a local high school running track. The sun was shining, but a breeze prevented the evening from becoming too warm. A stage had been erected on one side of the track, and upbeat music, sometimes country and sometimes rock 'n roll, blasted from the on-stage speakers. Scattered around the track, tents had been pitched by various groups of people. The groups, made up of adults and children of all ages, wore matching t-shirts, signifying their individual team memberships. Some sported tie-dye, others pink or white or blue. The largest group wore purple—this year a heather purple, which pleased me because that was my group... the survivors.

There were warm greetings among the survivors, genuinely happy to see one another. We gathered under the largest tent for a meal of sandwiches, fruit, and cookies. We laughed and reminisced, living in the moment, a skill that many survivors have perfected. We stood for the national anthem and then a prayer.

There were various speeches and introductions. Event organizers, beautiful and caring people who had obviously dedicated a tremendous amount of time and effort, were greeted with hearty applause. And people who had raised varying amounts of impressive and generous donations and sponsorships were also enthusiastically applauded. Luminarias, hundreds of them individually decorated, were lining the track, waiting to be lit as the sun set. We had gathered for the annual Relay for Life.

Lasting 18 hours each year, The Relay for Life is a fund-raising event sponsored by the American Cancer Society. It takes place worldwide during daylight and overnight. As darkness descends upon the track, it is a reminder of the physical effects, emotions, and mental state of cancer patients undergoing treatment. The fatigue experienced by relayers in the early morning hours mimics that of a cancer patient facing diagnosis, treatment, and recovery. The track is lined by luminarias, made in remembrance of those that have lost their fight against cancer, and in honor of those that are still fighting. Perhaps my favorite part of the Relay, each year I make one in remembrance of my dad.

But as much as I appreciate the support, camaraderie, and efforts of the event planners and my fellow survivors, The Relay for Life is a bittersweet experience for me. Please don't misunderstand—I am extremely appreciative of the funds that are raised by more than 4 million relay participants worldwide. And I am honored to be treated, along with my fellow survivors, as a VIP each year. And although each year that I attend, I am very glad that I did, it is a reminder of the loved ones I have lost and of the battle that I continue to fight.

This year my role was a little different than in years past. Along with receiving my medal, walking the Survivor Lap, and seeing a luminary meant for me, this year I would be the Survivor Speaker. I had been asked to talk about what it means to be a survivor. Although my speech was to be only about five minutes in length, I found this to be a challenging assignment. My definition of survivor has changed over the past eight years; it has become more defined, and it carries a great deal of emotional and spiritual weight. Following is the recording* of my speech. I have also included the transcript because although I think that speeches are better heard than read, I realize that the recording may not work for everyone (some of us would rather be quilting than figuring out computer technology). I believe that it conveys my message about what it means to be a survivor. And as I spoke, I could see survivors in the audience nodding their heads in agreement and wiping away tears. Hopefully I represented them well.

Here's to my fellow survivors! ~Kelly~

Relay for Life Survivor Speech 2015

"I am excited and honored to be here this evening and especially excited to be speaking to my fellow survivors. Whether just diagnosed with cancer, in treatment, in remission, or cured, we are all survivors. We began to learn to be survivors from the time we were born, and we were survivors the moment that first cancer cell showed up in our bodies. We were survivors yesterday, we are survivors today, and we will be survivors tomorrow.

I didn't always feel that way. When I was diagnosed with cancer 8 years ago, I didn't want to be a part of this—didn't want to be here. I wanted to hide, and I wanted to deny that I had cancer. I wanted to get through treatment as quickly as I could, be cured, and put the whole thing behind me. I just wanted my life to go back to normal. I'm sure that many survivors feel the same way.

But as I contemplate what it means to be a survivor, I am reminded of a quote by William Bennett: "This is our story—about going from one world into another, and the attitudes and dispositions with which we face that new world. It's about choosing smiles over tears and effort over complaint or regret." And as I contemplate that quote, and again what it means to be a survivor, I am reminded of what I have learned from my journey with cancer. I have learned a couple of very important things.

First, I have learned that I couldn't walk away as if nothing had ever happened because cancer changes us—it changes our bodies, our health, our spirits, and our lives. But, among those changes, cancer has made me stronger, more determined, and better prepared. It has made me appreciate each day more than ever before, and it has made me braver than I have ever been. It has made my faith more profound, and it has taught me to love more deeply. What I have learned is that although I couldn't run away from cancer, and my life would certainly not go back to normal, I could choose to turn toward the places where I find inspiration, and I could choose the way in which I carry out this journey.

We, as survivors, choose the way in which we carry out this journey. We could choose to wallow in self-pity and become blind to the beauty of each day. And we could choose to be fearful, controlled by anxiety and an unknown future. However, as survivors, we have chosen to face each day with optimism and courage. We have chosen to rely on our faith and the faith of those who love us and believe in us. We have chosen to set an example of resilience for our children and grandchildren, our brothers and sisters, our friends and our communities. And we have chosen hope over fear, "smiles over tears and effort over complaint or regret."

I have also learned that survivorship is not a solo act. We have not survived alone, and we are surrounded by our co-survivors—our loved ones, our families, our friends, our caretakers, and our communities. Without their love, support, and encouragement, we are merely getting by. But with our co-survivors, we don't face this journey alone. We have someone beside us, driving us to appointments, sitting with us throughout treatment, shouldering the bad news and the good. We have someone bringing meals when we aren't up to cooking, running errands for us, and looking out for our children. Our co-survivors make an evening such as this possible. They celebrate with us and for us. They also choose "smiles over tears and effort over complaint or regret."

So, how do we carry out this journey, this story of ours? How do we face this new world? Well, as survivors we dig deep, we pluck up our courage, we pull ourselves up by the boot straps, and we put one foot in front of the other. We buck up, we take the bull by the horns, and we get back in the saddle... And most of all we never, ever, ever give up."

(* The audio of Kelly's speech can be found on YouTube. ~Erin)

6. ME AND MY CO-STARS

On July 29, 2015

Cancer didn't take me by surprise, not really. I remember suspecting that I had it. Not like a hypochondriac suspects a myriad of diseases based on a few vague symptoms. It was more like a dawning realization. Like most health care professionals, I know enough to be dangerous to myself and for a few months in the spring of 2007, I just didn't feel right. But I had been training for a triathlon, pushing myself with lengthy miles in a bike saddle, lap after lap in the pool, and long, lonely runs along ditch banks. I told myself that I had been training too hard, that my body was adjusting to the changes I had made in my diet, and that the dietary supplements I had recently started were likely culprits. But I remember that early spring morning when I figured it out. It was dark, not even 5am, as I drove to the Y for an early swim before getting the girls off to school. Something in my mind clicked, the pieces fell into place, and for a moment I experienced a panicky feeling that made me feel lonelier than I had ever been. To this day, I avoid making that drive in the wee hours of the morning because it causes me to relive that sensation—that KNOWING something serious was about to happen, something so big that my life would change forever, something that no one could get me out of.

Cancer is a solo act. It's just you—there's no understudy, no replacement, no substitute... or so I thought. True, only you go through treatment; only you wade through the numerous side effects; only you choke down pills designed to control those side effects. Alone, you lie awake at night, praying for a little more time, for strength to face another round of chemo, for a miracle. But in reality, we aren't alone. And if we allow ourselves to reach out, to connect, and to be held up, we find that we are surrounded by the inspiration we receive from others.

When I was originally diagnosed, treatment included radiation along with chemotherapy. Every day for a month, I lay on a table in a mold made specifically to fit my body, hidden beyond a giant lead door, positioned just right so that the radiation beams lined up properly with the little black dots that had been tattooed onto my abdomen. And every day as I sat in the radiation waiting area, I chatted with an older gentleman also waiting for his few minutes on the table beyond the lead door. As we became acquainted, I learned that he drove quite a distance to receive treatment, he lived alone, and his grown children lived far away. Over time, a friendship of sorts began, and when we discovered that we would each finish radiation on the same day, we made a date to celebrate with ice cream. Unwilling to admit this would be a difficult task for each of us, we talked about our ice cream date with anticipation. My friend's radiation targeted his jaw and neck, making it difficult and painful to swallow. Mine targeted my abdomen and pelvis, making my gut ache and causing me to lose interest in food. But I believe that the human spirit was prevailing, making us feel brave and confident in our camaraderie. Although I never saw my friend again after our radiation ended, I learned an important lesson—the power of inspiration we gain from the relationships that surround us.

I'm really a very private person—which I realize is ironic for someone with a blog that journals a very personal and life-changing experience. In fact, when I was originally diagnosed, I was secretive about it. It was as though I could control it—as though the cancer would not take over my life if I held it close. I suppose I was also protecting my children. They were so young, and I didn't want them to be afraid. I was wrong about all of that, and over time, I learned that the way we connect with one another, the way we reach out to one another, is incredibly strengthening, soothing, and empowering. It lets us know that the solo act isn't quite so solo, and in reality, we have lots of co-stars.

It's my mother, who has sat in exam rooms and stoically shouldered bad news alongside me. It's my sister who picks me up when I'm down and frequently reminds me that I'm not done fighting yet. It's my brother-in-law, who last fall, during my really dark days and even darker nights said, "If you feel anxious in the night, just call out to me. That's why I'm here."

It's my daughters who are so resilient and mature beyond their years, having had a mother with cancer more than half their young lives.

It's my boyfriend who willingly and without complaint takes on every project and chore at my home—I believe at times just to see me smile.

It's my friends who have driven me to appointments, brought meals to my home, sent cards and emails, left phone and text messages, and hugged me in my kitchen. They drive by, pull in to the driveway and stop to chat a bit. They offer to irrigate the horse pasture, stack hay in the barn, and make sure my girls have a ride home from school. On Facebook, friends I've not seen in decades, cheer me on through even the smallest of achievements.

It's the strangers who upon seeing that I'm chemo-bald, approach me in a store or on a plane or at an event and ask if I'm fighting cancer. And when I've confirmed their suspicions, they ask if they can hug me and pray for me. They take my hand in theirs and share their experiences as warriors alongside me.

It's the professionals, now friends, who have cared for me for eight long years. Who have cheered my treatment successes and have grieved when treatment failed. It's my nurses who so competently keep me safe during treatment, my oncologist who reminds me that I'm in a marathon, not a sprint, and my social worker who allows me to voice my fears and mourn my losses yet magically steers me back to my strengths and the pleasure I find in every day adventures.

It's my former patients who I run into at the grocery store and the gas station and the school, who tell me they've missed me and want me to know that if I need anything, help with anything, anything at all…

So as I reflect on the past eight years, the disappointments and the triumphs, I acknowledge that something big did happen—something that would indeed forever change my life. I learned that by reaching out, sharing the experience, and allowing others in on it, I would find inspiration. I also learned that what I thought would be a solo act, has never been so.

Here's to my co-stars ~Kelly~

7. POLLYANNA AND HER PITY PARTY

September 8, 2015

I am not a Pollyanna. In fact, I happen to have a standing invitation to a one-woman pity party at which I am the guest of honor. Although I've never been one to miss a party, I do work hard to avoid this one. Instead, I focus on inspiration, live in the moment, and try very hard to cultivate hope.

I know how very fragile hope can be. I know that hope often balances precariously, held up by thin threads of human spirit, easily snapped by something as innocent as a few words or as daunting as the truth. I know that hope can easily come crashing down.

Yesterday I sat in a hospital bed at the National Cancer Institute in Bethesda, Maryland, waiting for the results of multiple tests—blood work, chest X-ray, EKG, brain MRI, CT scan of my chest, abdomen, and pelvis. My future, along with the opportunity to participate in a potentially cancer curing clinical trial, hung in limbo, dependent on the results of these many tests. There was a knock on the door, and the medical team entered the room. Physicians, nurses, researchers surrounded my bed. The lead physician, a handsome and compassionate young man, already vested in my welfare, pulled up a chair next to the bed. Quietly he sat down and looked at me intently. And in that moment, my hope was shattered.

There would be no clinical trial for me. It turns out the cancer has spread to my brain, forcing me to be dismissed from the trial. Due to the metastasis lurking in my gray matter, the risks of the trial treatment now outweigh the potential benefits. Instead I will go home, regroup, and begin radiation. And I will rally.

But not yet. For now, I'm in shock by this unexpected and devastating news. My mind is in denial, preventing me from absorbing the whole truth with its many implications.

After the medical team left my room, some with tears on their cheeks, I let down my delicate veil of courage and dignity, and I held my head in my hands and I wept. I wept for myself and the loss of my fragile hope. And I wept for my daughters, my mother and sister and the family and friends who love me so and who will now have their hope shattered, too.

My mother and stepfather, sitting beside my bed and having witnessed the grave delivery of news, also cried. But when we were done, after they had wrapped their arms around me and we had prayed, my stepdad said, "Do you still want to go out for crab and shrimp tonight?" And I looked at him and said "Hell yes!," which caused him to chuckle and Mom and I to smile.

For a bit, I would not indulge in the pity party. For a bit, I would push it aside, opting instead to partake in my favorite east coast meal at a Maryland restaurant—a true treat for an Idaho gal. For a bit, and as often as possible, eventually and once again extending to most of the time, I will live in the moment. I will practice the art of mindfulness as best I can. And with that, I will again find inspiration.

Four years ago, when I was originally told that this cancer is incurable, I grieved. And, as I grieved, my mind raced with uncontrollable thoughts and visions of an unknown future that did not include me. Most of the thoughts were about my three daughters and how their stories would unfold without me. And the grief that my death would cause them. My thoughts were also about how much I enjoy this world, this life, and how I wasn't ready to give up the small stuff—the smell of fresh cut hay, the sight of sun glistening on water, the sound of my daughters' laughter. These thoughts spiraled out of control, paralyzing me with fear and bathing me in overwhelming sadness.

It was at that time a psychiatrist specializing in cancer patients introduced me to the concept of mindfulness. She explained that by projecting myself into the future and allowing my thoughts to be out of control, I wasn't really present in the here and now. I was essentially robbing myself of being present in the current moment. This made sense to me, and desperate to regain control of my mind and to feel joy again, I latched onto the theory for dear life. After leaving her office that day, I detoured to a bookstore to further immerse myself in the concept of mindfulness. I was especially interested in the writings of Dr. Jon Kabat-Zinn, an expert in mindfulness. A professor at the University of Massachusetts Medical School, Dr. Kabat-Zinn has integrated mind/body science with meditation, relaxation, and self-healing techniques. I sensed that if I could consume and master this concept, I could live more comfortably within the confines of incurable cancer and could once again find pleasure, even adventure, in each day.

It has taken practice and self-discipline to become good at mindfulness. And sometimes, such as today in the wake of devastating news, I battle with myself to rein in the frightening thoughts. But in doing so, I am less stressed, less sad, and am more focused, more joyful. I am able to reconnect with my surroundings and the relationships that are so important to me. I am able to truly live in the moment and appreciate the small and beautiful things that life has to offer—a cup of tea on the front porch, a conversation with my daughters on the way to school, the familiar scent of my horse as I hug his neck. Mindfulness allows me many, many moments, extending into minutes, hours and even whole days, when I'm able to forget that I'm a cancer patient.

So, I'm going home, and I will rally. I've already contacted my beloved medical team and a plan of attack is forming. They will take good care of me. Family and friends will surround me and hold me up. The prayer chains will continue. And although I will likely visit the pity party from time to time over the next few days, I won't stay long. Instead, I will ditch the party in favor of mindfulness and will once again find pleasure, joy, and adventure in each day. In fact, I'm already looking forward to watching my daughter play her trumpet in the marching band on Friday night. And I have a couple of quilts in mind—fabrics, colors, and patterns are dancing in my head. I think I'll go through my stash and get started this weekend.

Here's to living in the moment ~Kelly~

8. MY DAUGHTER IS A GRAPPLER

September 30, 2015

My teenage daughter is a grappler. She wrestles. And in Idaho that means that during the high school season, she wrestles both boys and girls—very few girls and lots of boys well on their way to manhood. During the freestyle season, she wrestles more girls, and we travel to all-girl tournaments, where the competition is both serious and fierce.

When my daughter was in the eighth grade, she informed me that she would like to start wrestling. Being unfamiliar with the sport, my immediate response was an emphatic no. I explained that I didn't want her to compete in a "boys' sport." I told her that I saw no value in it. But after the initial surprise and upon further reflection—I suppose influenced, at least in part, by a life altered by cancer—I decided that she, rather than I, should determine the experiences she would have in life. And so I relented and told her that she could wrestle... I warned her it would be difficult, would require a great deal of self-discipline... and courage. And she would be required to agree to my rules.

Rule 1: No quitting. If you start the season, you must finish the season. No matter how difficult it is and whether you find success or failure, you will not quit.

Rule 2: Never cry on the mat. I have seen boys cry on the mat. Leave that for them. You may need to find a quiet corner later, after your match, but do not be a girl that cries on the mat.

Rule 3: Do not expect preferential treatment because you are a girl. Just because you have chosen a sport dominated by boys does not mean that you should expect to be treated differently because you are a girl. In fact, if anything, you will need to work harder to demonstrate that you are serious and a true competitor.

Rule 4: Above all, you must maintain your femininity. Just because you have chosen to participate in a male-dominated sport does not mean that you should compromise yourself or try to be something that you're not.

My daughter agreed to my rules, and next month she will begin her third season of wrestling. It's safe to say that she has learned a great deal about self-discipline, strength, courage, and fitness. She has learned the self-satisfying excitement of winning as well as the humbling disappointment of losing. She now knows the strength gained from the support of her teammates and the thrill of a sport in which two competitors, alone on the mat, face off. She has even become competitive on the national level. At the end of her first high school season, as her coach was making remarks about each wrestler at the season banquet, he described her, the only girl on the team, as brave. I could not have been more proud.

Nearly a month ago I was forced to grapple as well. I was faced with shocking and frightening news and had to wrestle with the knowledge that cancer had metastasized to my brain. Once the initial shock wore off, I realized that I had to face my challenge. I could even say I performed a mental take down, and today I completed the match—I finished a course of radiation designed to annihilate those lesions. As I lay on the radiation table, my head bolted in place so that I could not move, so that the radiation beams would be accurate within a millimeter, my mind wandered, and I found myself thinking about my daughter, the wrestler.

I thought about the stoic manner in which she has approached her self-induced challenge, and I thought about the four rules that I had imposed upon her. As I lay there with invisible beams penetrating my skull, it occurred to me that those four simple rules apply to life. A life well lived does not allow for quitting, for crying on the mat, for expecting preferential treatment, or for forgetting who we are. A life well lived requires strength, courage, faith, and desire.

As we prepare for another season of wrestling—nine months in all—another season of bouts and take downs, throws and pins, wins and losses, I do not need to remind my daughter of my four rules. She knows them well. She lives them.~ Kelly~

9. THE ALL-TRUE ADVENTURES OF KELLY ON CHEMO

November 17, 2015

Ugh. Yuck. Puke. After a six-month hiatus, I am back on chemotherapy. I hate chemo—it addles my brain and sickens my body. And then there are the side effects of the drugs used to control the chemo side effects. My daughters joke that I am familiar with every public restroom within a 100-mile radius. I have strange (and probably disgusting) food cravings while on chemo. And I can vomit on command. I am about to be bald for the fifth time in eight years—this time hoping to keep my eyebrows and eyelashes because I'm just not very good at applying the fake ones. I recall a lunch date with two dear friends during which I'm quite sure one set of eyelashes was in danger of dropping into my pasta salad. They were both too kind to comment.

At the same time, I must be grateful. I am aware that chemotherapy has kept me alive. I have joked that I am a chemo addict, showing up at the clinic praying that my blood counts would be high enough to allow another infusion, practically begging my dear doctor not to lower my dose, and outright lying about the severity of side effects. Hearing loss? Ringing in my ears? Not a problem. Numbness in my feet? Hardly. Diarrhea? Not to speak of. Nausea and vomiting? Minor issue. Fatigue? Shortness of breath? Only when I run. I'm quite sure he's on to me.

In truth, cancer and its myriad treatments have trapped me in a body that I no longer recognize. That's a bold statement, and I have friends and acquaintances that certainly have a greater claim to that sentiment than I do. I suppose some of it may mimic the aging process. If so, it's in fast forward, and I wasn't prepared to give it up so soon. I was once an athlete. Heck, in my mind I still am. I ran and swam and biked and skied. I rode my horse with abandon, and I was strong. I carried three pregnancies and delivered each one naturally. With the third, I drove myself to the hospital, blowing between contractions, reassuring my three-year-old daughter bouncing along in the pickup with me, and delivering 11 minutes after arriving. I had the strength to stack hay bales and the endurance to swim and bike a half ironman. But the body that did all of that no longer exists. And with that loss, my sense of adventure has changed.

There was a time when I thought of adventure as riding a horse through the Swiss Alps, dancing in the streets of Paris on Bastille Day, and skiing the ungroomed slopes of Alaska. With friends, I ventured into Mexican border towns for evenings of dance, laughter, and late-night swims in the Colorado River. And for years, along with a group of equally thrill-seeking cowgirls, I fed my adrenaline addiction by riding my steel-gray quarter horse at breakneck speeds through rodeo arenas.

I suppose in all fairness, my idea of adventure changed somewhat when I became a mother. As a mother, I found adventure through the eyes of my children and the wonder with which they viewed everyday happenings. As they grew, teaching them to do the things I have loved so much—swim, bike, ski, ride—became an opportunity to relive the excitement. I learned that adventure is much, much more than exotic places, thrill seeking, and adrenaline. Motherhood taught me that adventure takes place without ever leaving home. And although given the opportunity I would still gladly zip line through a South American jungle, snorkel off the coast of Mexico, and parasail over an aqua-colored ocean, I've also learned to find adventure every day and all around me.

More than ever I appreciate the adventure found in the kinship of family and friends. Together we share the challenges, celebrate the triumphs, and measure the milestones. We embrace one another through laughter and tears. We encourage, congratulate, and console. With each new day offering unchartered territory, we are life's explorers, sightseeing, searching, and discovering.

I still ride my beloved horse. Of course, he is much older now, too, so we both prefer to just mosey down the trail. His gentle cadence rises through my saddle, easing tension from my back and shoulders, allowing me to reflect on the many miles we have covered together. Although I require frequent hot chocolate breaks, I still ski the mountains of Idaho. I am stimulated by the majestic views from the chair lift and the sound of my skis on fresh snow. And I can still swim and bike now and then but the real adventure for me is in watching my daughters at a swim meet or completing their first triathlon.

Last fall, when my future appeared to be especially bleak, and I was feeling like I just hadn't experienced enough adventures on this earth, I decided to try something new. It had all the makings of adventure... new skills, new knowledge, some excitement, and maybe even a little risk. I decided I would create a quilt for each of my daughters. Hoping to live long enough to meet my goal, I immersed myself in this new adventure. I learned the pleasure to be gained from the camaraderie of fellow quilters, the excitement of expressing my creativity, and the challenge of acquiring new skills. And, of course, I learned the self-satisfaction of having met my goal and presenting each of my daughters with a beautiful finished product, complete with errors that made it uniquely my creation. On the back of each quilt, I added a secret pocket into which I slipped hand written notes. My notes told the girls why I had chosen their particular quilt pattern and fabrics and what the experience had meant for me. Since then, I have made several more quilts. Each is unique, and although I do plenty of seam ripping, with each I have found solace.

I believe that the strength and endurance that were mine in a life before cancer have served me well. I believe they have helped me, perhaps even inspired me, to withstand the rigors of cancer treatment. I know that they have allowed me to be inspired by my new-found form of adventure. And I am so very grateful for all of it.

Adventure on! ~Kelly~

10. BALD IS BEAUTIFUL

February 5, 2016

I told myself that it doesn't matter, that I don't care, and that I won't cry. But I guess it does matter and I do care because I did cry as I watched handfuls of hair swirling around my ankles and plugging the shower drain.

This is the fifth time that I've lost my hair to chemotherapy, and really I'm used to it. I've learned that my bald head has a pretty good shape to it and that having no hair is surprisingly liberating. Although it helps to wear bold earrings and eye enhancing makeup, for a woman to be bald is so honest and open. I have acquired a beautiful stash of scarves and head-wraps, and thanks to YouTube, I've learned to tie them in fashionable styles. In some ways, having no hair simplifies my life. Tying a scarf or scrunching a soft head-wrap onto my noggin is much easier and faster than drying and curling or sitting in a salon chair. Of course, there is the issue of having just the right color to go with whatever outfit I have planned. But just today a fellow chemo patient complimented the head-wrap I'm wearing—a silky black number with swirls of bright blue throughout. I promised her I would make one for her.

So I don't think I'm vain about my hair loss. I think instead that the hair loss and ensuing sadness and tears symbolize something else for me. They symbolize the multiple losses that cancer has created in my life. Because of cancer I've lost freedom. Instead my life is governed by the appointments that are necessary for blood tests, CT scans, MRIs, chemotherapy, blood transfusions, and visits with my oncologist. Before I can plan anything, I have to consider where I will be in my chemo cycle and whether or not I will feel well enough to attend an event, go on a trip, or participate in an activity. Because of cancer I've lost strength and endurance and therefore many of the activities that I once enjoyed, like distance swimming, mountain biking, and long days of gardening. Because of cancer I've lost much of the career that I worked so hard to build and that I loved so much. With that, I have lost stimulating and challenging interactions with colleagues and students, and I have lost rewarding, tender moments with patients. And because of cancer I have lost some of my independence, which spans from financial freedom to the day-to-day functioning of my household. But most of all, and the loss that I mourn the most, is my innocence.

I believe that there are aspects of life to which we are, and will hopefully remain, innocent. I have a sense that the human spirit can rise, prevail, and remain optimistic, at least in part, because we can be innocent to the trials, crises, and pain that await us. We begin our stint in this world with complete innocence and although life events strip it away over time, it is a gift worth nurturing for as long as possible. But cancer has robbed me of my innocence. It left me, quickly and without ceremony, but gone nevertheless.

When I hear that a friend or relative or someone in my close-knit community has received a new diagnosis of cancer, I mourn the loss of innocence that I know awaits them. As my own innocence left me, it was replaced with an uninvited insight. I learned to bravely shoulder bad news, saving my grief for the privacy of a parking lot. I became familiar with physical and emotional pain at a level that I had not known before. I learned to navigate hospitals and clinics intimately and to aggressively advocate for myself. I know what chemotherapy and radiation really feel like and how far I'm willing to go to survive. I know what it is to forego all dignity and travel thousands of miles to beg a cancer researcher to not give up on me, to not forget me, to consider me a candidate for his next clinical trial because the previous one failed. I know what it's like to discuss a future that doesn't include me, to literally plan my funeral so that no one else will have to, and most painful of all, to prepare my children for a life without me. Uninvited insight has shown me what's it's like to watch life from the sidelines—like a movie preview——getting a taste of what I won't be around to witness.

But it doesn't stop there. Although I have paid with my innocence, I also recognize that uninvited insight has given me a depth of knowledge and a better understanding than I had in my life before cancer. I have unwittingly received life altering lessons of grace and love and courage. I have learned that I am stronger than I ever realized, willing to withstand just about anything to lengthen my time on this earth. I have learned that I am a good mother and that even at their tender ages, I have raised daughters that are resilient and brave, kind and loving. I have learned that whether I am living or not, they will look out for one another, they will have good lives, and they will be alright. I have learned that there is indeed power in prayer and that spiritual growth is abundant during times of fear and suffering and deepest desire. I have learned to be the humble recipient of the kindness of strangers, meeting their open arms and appreciating every encouraging word and comforting deed. I have learned how truly blessed I am to have family and friends willing to drop everything to come to my rescue, to prod me along when I become doubtful, providing a kinship that defies description. I have learned to slow down, to recognize my priorities, to perfect the art of living in the moment, and to find the beauty, even for fleeting moments, in each and every day that is given to me.

Perhaps these are lessons that I should have learned earlier in life and at a lower price. I knew I was loved, that God does great things, and that the kinships I enjoy run deep. But I think that my innocence allowed me to take it all for granted, to know but not know, to lull myself into false security, and to assume it would last forever. It was the loss of innocence and the arrival of uninvited insight that taught me to whittle away at the superfluous and to focus instead on what is most important to me—God, motherhood, family, and friends. It taught me to narrow my focus and to take advantage of opportunities that might enrich the lives of those I care about as well as my own. That is not to say that I have given up on frivolity. Goodness no! Frivolity is a part of my adventures, woven into my daily life, soothing my soul, and entertaining my mind. Frivolity induces hysterical laughter with my daughters over jokes that only we can understand. It encourages my mind to creatively wander, planning flower beds, decorating for holidays, and playing the piano as if for an audience. Frivolity seduces me into creating quilts beyond my ability level, exploring methods and styles as if I've quilted for decades.

And so, as I mourn the loss of my innocence while drying tears over lost hair and find solace in yet another quilt block, one might wonder, if I could be cured, would I give up cancer? In a heartbeat. But would I reclaim my innocence in trade for what cancer has given me? Never. ~Kelly~

11. IT'S COMPLICATED

April 12, 2016

Not so long ago I unexpectedly found myself in the emergency room of our local hospital. I guess that's a silly statement—nearly all visits to the emergency room are unexpected. For several days, I hadn't been feeling well, exhibiting symptoms that I was sure were pneumonia—fatigue, shortness of breath, cough, and sometimes a fever accompanied by night sweats. None of that was so out of the ordinary for a cancer patient, and it wasn't enough to coax this veteran of healthcare into the ER. Oh no, instead I waited until my heart suddenly felt like it was jumping out of my chest, reaching an unsustainable rate of 225 beats per minute. Only then was I ready to admit that I needed medical attention.

Luckily, when my heart began misbehaving, I was already in town, having just dropped my daughter off at swim team practice. Riding along in my pickup truck, I quietly tried to valsalva my heart back to a normal sinus rhythm. That didn't work. So then I found a still packaged drinking straw from a long forgotten fast food meal and tried to breathe through that. But it was to no avail, and my heart remained in what I had by then self-diagnosed as atrial fibrillation. Never having experienced such a thing before, I was mildly curious as to why and much more curious as to how long this chest pounding discomfort would continue.

Once in the ER I received a myriad of tests—blood work, ECG, constant vital signs, and a chest X-ray that I assured the ER staff would be ugly, because, after all that is where the cancer now resides. Checking on me frequently, the very kind, competent, and concerned ER physician finally informed me that along with the atrial fibrillation that I had accurately self-diagnosed, I also had some sort of pneumonia, as well as dehydration, and severe anemia. In fact, periodic tests revealed that the anemia continued to worsen, perhaps indicating a grave and often fatal condition. As if that wasn't enough, he also told me that my potassium level was much too low and that I appeared to be having what could be a thyroid storm. I would need to be admitted to the hospital for IV antibiotics, a hefty blood transfusion, continuous oxygen, re-hydration, more tests, and consults with specialists. And perhaps to me the most disturbing of all, I would need to be transferred by ambulance to a bigger hospital in a bigger city because I was just "too complicated."

TOO COMPLICATED?!?!?!?! I cracked the physician's carefully composed demeanor a little when I blurted out that "I never wanted to be one of THOSE patients."

But I had become one of THOSE patients, and I found myself waiting for the ambulance and for my critical care bed to be readied at the big city hospital.

It was only then that I acknowledged that I was facing a crisis and that I would need to draw from my sources of inspiration. With desperation seeping into my mind, I searched for every truth I've known, everything I've written about, every source of strength I've experienced, every point of hope, every lingering connection I have to this earth. I prayed, begging God to wrap his arms around me and to fill my heart with His love and courage. I focused on my three daughters, my desire to continue to be their mother, and how much I don't want to let them down. By then, my family had begun to gather in the ER, and I looked into my own mother's face as she leaned over my hospital gurney to whisper to me. I found myself hanging on the loving, encouraging words of the woman who brought me into this world, nurtured me, and who I know has prayed to take my place as a cancer patient.

While I waited for the ambulance, I watched the anxious, loving family members who had gathered to rally around me, to protect me, and to comfort one another in the wake of yet another cancer-induced moment of truth. My three beautiful daughters were there.

My amazing sister and loyal brother-in-law were there along with my loving mom and stepdad. And my boyfriend, who was doing his best to keep me calm, holding my hand and practically tap dancing in an attempt to ease the tension, was there. And as I watched them—talking to one another, occasionally laughing at a private joke, or covertly watching my heart monitor, I realized that I was looking at my world. All that matters to me. Everything. And that is not complicated at all.

It's really very simple. With everything stripped away, facing my own mortality and an uncertain immediate future, I realize (and have for quite some time) that these relationships are really all that matters. When all else is gone or taken, we still have love.

Later, during the ambulance ride to Boise, my heart rate spontaneously converted back to a normal sinus rhythm. Perhaps it was the gentle bouncing of the ambulance; perhaps it was the lively conversation that the paramedic and I had about our presidential candidates, or perhaps it was thoughts of the unfinished quilt that awaited on my sewing machine, expecting me home to align the seams and add the remaining few blocks. Whatever the case, it felt really good and I was able to relax a little.

Although I remained in the hospital for a few days, I quickly improved. The pneumonia and anemia were treated, blood tests leveled out, and my heart continued to behave itself. The possibly fatal condition detected in the ER did not progress. And most importantly, I learned that what really matters is not complicated at all. ~Kelly~

12. A LOVING TRIBUTE TO A SOURCE OF INSPIRATION

April 17, 2016

God knew I would need a sister, and so He gave me one. Today, although she is two thousand and forty five point six miles away, I honor my sister and celebrate her birthday.

My "little" sister was born when I was just 18 months old. The day my parents brought her home from the hospital I announced that she was "my baby." And we have been close companions, comrades, and confidantes ever since.

We have shared bedrooms, toys, and friends. We have shared adventures and misadventures, joy and grief, success and failure. We have traveled the world together, been the new kids at school together, and got caught up in mischief together. We have protected one another from teasing and tattling and comforted one another when protection wasn't enough.

As children, we played board games for hours; Clue, Sorry, and Monopoly marathons occupied our time on rainy Sunday afternoons. We created intricate scenarios for our Barbie dolls and watched Saturday morning cartoons, sharing Pop Tarts and Cap'n Crunch.

We danced in the living room to Simon and Garfunkel and later to Foreigner and Motown. Together we learned to swim, our years on the swim team favorite memories that began lessons in strength and endurance and forged lifetime friendships. Together we learned to play the piano, sharing duets, suffering through one another's wrong notes and missed chords, and practicing the increasingly complicated sonatas, concertos, and occasional jazz. Together we galloped bareback through the orchards, clinging to each other, and giggling as we pulled one another from our horse's broad back, the tall grasses softening our fall and muffling our laughter. In our head-to-toe matching outfits, together we learned to navigate the ski slopes, a skill that she took to an even greater level, never shying away from the challenge of a mogul field or backcountry skiing. As we grew older, we joined the high school track and cross-country teams, our much admired coach inspiring further strength and endurance that we believe serve in my cancer fight today. We tossed rifles, spun flags, and danced on the drill team together, attracted by the sequined outfits, way-cool white boots, and the cute drummers in the marching band. Later still, we lived together in college, joining the same sorority, sharing our secret handshake, songs, and rituals, as well as a larger band of sisterhood that would someday also be a source of inspiration. We spent summers together in the humidity of the Deep South and the midnight sun of the Alaskan Interior, working, exploring, and maturing those many miles from home.

We have shared secrets and jokes, laughing until we cried over silly things that only sisters could understand. And as if all of that wasn't enough, she gave me an incredible brother-in-law who understands and supports our sister bond.

She proposed that I compete in my first triathlon—and then joined me and led the way. She has scouted quilting shops for me, encouraging my new-found hobby. She shares her writing with me, often before an editor sees her work for the first time. She rocked my first baby, so that I could sleep. She stood beside me when I married and was beside me when my marriage failed. She provided a name for my second daughter, her namesake. She is the godmother of my three daughters. She is the executor of my estate. I miss her when we are apart. She is the person I trust most in the world.

I can't imagine my life without my sister, my constant companion, my greatest cheerleader. And for the past 8 years, as I've faced my life's biggest challenge, it is largely my sister that keeps me going. She has traveled this country with me in search of treatment; she has celebrated treatment success and grieved treatment failure. She has spent long days at hospital bedsides, driven me to and from chemo and radiation, waited for a surgeon's news, and attended appointments so that I need not face the unknown alone. She has turned her life upside down to be with my children when I couldn't be. She has stayed with me so that my household could function even when I could not. When I am down and feeling hopeless, she encourages me, logically and calmly reminding me that my fight is not finished. She has put her own needs and desires on hold. All for me.

I would like to think that all siblings enjoy this degree of love and commitment from one another. But I realize how very blessed I am. Heck, with all of those gifts you would think it's my birthday, rather than hers, that I celebrate today. Luckily for me, and for the many people who know and love my sister, it is her birthday. I hope that as a sister, I provide to her even a small amount of what she does for me, and every day I thank God for giving me the sister He knew I would need. And now I really should finish the quilt I've started for her! Happy birthday, Erin! ~Love, Kelly~

13. GUILT IS MY FREQUENT COMPANION, HITCHHIKING THROUGH MY LIFE

September 8, 2016

Although I've not written for a while, my blog is frequently on my mind with ideas, experiences, and observations dancing through my head. Having become a silent but comforting confidante, I am unable to abandon my blog... As I drive through the countryside or lie awake in bed, I write in my head, creating descriptions and passages, explanations and scenarios. But for some reason, for the past few months, I've been unable to put it all together. It's not at all a lack of desire. Rather it has been a lack of focus and perhaps even energy. I have to carefully choose where and when to use my focus and energy, knowing that each is limited, and that I have to prioritize. But today I recognized, with the help of an insightful friend, that writing and blogging are actually a great source of inspiration for me and that without it, I'm feeling lost and disoriented within my own cancer journey... I feel as though I've gone astray. And to have lost my way just serves to compound this overwhelming and frightening experience. So today I'm back, intending to remain so, and ready to explore a subject that has been haunting me since I was diagnosed with cancer more than eight years ago... Guilt.

Guilt is my frequent companion, unexpected and uninvited. It pops up from time to time, hitchhiking through my life, an ugly visitor on an already difficult journey. I feel guilty for having cancer, for being terminally ill, for losing my ability to participate in life the way I once did. I feel guilty that people have to take care of me, clean up after me, and rearrange their own lives in order to accommodate my needs and my desires. I even feel guilty for the envy that I sometimes feel when I watch seemingly healthy people going about the daily activities of life—activities that are no longer a part of my repertoire—excitedly dashing up a flight of stairs to retrieve a forgotten item, energetically jogging down the road in pursuit of fitness, effortlessly maneuvering through the chores and tasks of the day. But most of all, I feel guilty because I am a mother with cancer and the lives of my children are forever and irreversibly changed by that ugly six-letter word.

My feelings of guilt have led me to apologize to my loved ones, my family and friends, on many occasions. I apologize when I have a particularly bad day, when my pain is out of control, and when I'm unable to participate in the simplest of activities—an evening meal, a short walk with the dogs, gathering eggs from the chicken coop. I apologize when my family has to carry me, doing the things I can no longer do because I'm too tired, too weak, or too slow. I apologize when I break down and become tearful, expressing my fears and anxieties, because I know that their love for me forces them along that ugly path of dread and angst right beside me. At the very least, I am aware that it is painful to watch me suffer, and for that I am, of course, sorry. And I apologize to my children for missing their special events, for asking them to take on even more responsibilities, and for worrying them on the days that I am too sad or too sick to properly mother them.

Of course, they all ask me why I apologize and tell me that I don't need to do so. I try to explain, to put into words this burdened state of mind and the sense that I am somehow responsible, at least in part, for the emotional well-being of those that care for me. But these feelings of guilt are complicated—my need to apologize, to express my regret, to clear my conscious, and to protect my loved ones from the ugly truth and far-reaching depth of this cancer—not fully understood even by me.

On a cognitive, conscious, and rational level I do know that I've done nothing wrong and that my feelings of guilt are unfounded. I didn't earn this cancer. No one, absolutely no one, deserves this. Nevertheless, I've made tremendous personal and financial sacrifices to pursue the best of cancer care. I've pushed my body and my sanity in search of treatment options and opportunities. I've learned firsthand the details, the good and the bad, of chemo, radiation, and surgery, clinical trials, nutritional options, and even acupuncture. I take better care of myself than ever before, realizing the benefits of light exercise, soothing naps, and pampering massage for cancer patients. And even as I pray, sometimes begging God to allow me more time, to make the pain stop, to help me find the strength I need to fight, and to heal my body, I am aware that I don't deserve this cancer or the myriad of burdens it has placed on my life. Neither do my loved ones. But for some reason, not completely appreciated by me, I do feel guilty.

Perhaps I sense that as these ugly little cellular mutations were taking place in my body, my own defense mechanisms were asleep at the wheel. When my body should have kicked into high gear to destroy the mutant cells, I might have been stressed or sleep deprived, causing my defenses to be otherwise occupied. Whatever the case, my body wasn't paying attention and it let me down. It left me in the lurch, deserted me in my hour of need, and it smacks of failure. And although I've made some impressive mistakes in my life, serious errors in judgment, I've never seen myself as a failure. I've generally accomplished what I set out to do, learning from my mistakes, and growing within my limitations. I've experienced success—as a mother, as a student, as a professional, as an athlete, as a woman. Until now. Now, as a mother with cancer, I feel as though I'm failing.

I once told a cancer psychiatrist about my feelings of guilt. I caught her off guard, and she was surprised by that revelation. I don't think she had considered that a victim of cancer might feel guilty. To her credit, she recovered well and then gave me much to think about. Ultimately, I have discovered that I'm not alone in these feelings of guilt. I've asked around. I've read up on it. Although none of us should, other cancer patients feel guilty, too.

Those of us in the cancer club find a multitude of reasons to blame ourselves for our predicament. We think we should have noticed our symptoms earlier, brought about an earlier diagnosis, and possibly found a more effective treatment. We are concerned that we are burdening our families and friends. And we worry about the welfare of those we might leave behind—especially the welfare of our children, their emotional health and physical comfort, a future for which we may not be present, and all of the life events that a mother can't bear to miss. We worry that lifestyle choices may have caused the cancer. Maybe we ate too much red meat, chugged too much milk, and slept too little. Maybe we didn't exercise enough, had one too many glasses of wine, or gave in to a sweet tooth too often. Maybe we lived in an exotic location where carcinogens traveled the water pipes, floated through the polluted air, or began as a parasitic virus. Maybe... If only... What if...

Bottom line, regardless of lifestyle, nutrition, sleeping habits, or living environment, no one deserves cancer. No one deserves the malignant mistakes made by our happy, little, normal cells as they copy DNA while they are growing and dividing. Heck, lots of people will live crazy, unhealthy, metamorphosis-inviting lifestyles and never have so much as a hint of a mutation. And although I've learned that I'm not alone in the I've-Got-Cancer-So-I-Feel-Guilty-Club, I've also learned that it's not healthy to dwell on guilt or on the past. Dwelling leads to anxiety and depression, and we wrangle with that enough as it is. Cancer is not our fault.

So as I try to ditch my uninvited companion, I'm working hard to let go of the maybes, if onlys, and what ifs. I focus on now. I focus on pleasure—whatever that may be—music, art, writing, companionship of family and friends, time spent with my daughters, and, of course, quilting. I focus on communion with God through prayer and scripture, conversations with my pastor, and spiritual readings. I focus on shared feelings, support from loved ones, and on the many positive aspects of my life for which I am thankful. And if the guilt continues, amid the apologies and regret, I must, we must, forgive ourselves. ~Kelly~

(Kelly passed away on October 8th, 2016, two days before her 52nd birthday and after more than eight years of battling cancer; yet, it's a war that she never truly lost—her courageous and joyous nature lives on in everyone who loved her. ~ Erin)

PART 2: A SISTER'S JOURNAL

1. PIG WHISPERER

The beige carpet blended with the walls, broken, perhaps, by a colorful print, but, sealed inside a shell of anxiety, I barely noticed my surroundings. Instead, I perched on the edge of an arm chair. A cup of juice and People magazine sat forgotten in front of me. All I could manage was to stare into space and mumble a string of prayers.

Although the oncology waiting room had been thoughtfully designed, from comfortable furniture to snacks and drinks to a pleasant staff, I might as well have been sitting in a dungeon rather than a basement. Waiting, after all, being a form of torture.

A clock ticked.

My heart hammered.

My sister Kelly finally emerged from behind a door. Alone. No smile. Questions formed an endless stream in my mind; yet, I could already guess the answers.

Kelly's tight-lipped expression spoke of a tentative control, emotions threatening to burst. I could tell she was relying on her dignity and stoicism to get her through this very public moment. But even after we'd emerged from the clinic into the shadows of the covered parking lot, she still hadn't spoken.

"What did the doctor say?" I blurted out, lacking her discipline.

She waved me off, and without a word, handed me the keys to her car. I slipped behind the steering wheel, while she crawled into the passenger side. I drove. The hospital shrank in my rearview mirror, until nothing was left, as if it had disappeared, gone forever, along with cancer, worry, and waiting.

I turned right and left, heading for the Interstate. Buildings, pedestrians, lights, and traffic blurred into a river of movement, so easy to drown oneself within the bustle of the city.

"There isn't a cure," Kelly said, a few minutes later.

I don't remember how I replied, somewhere between astonishment and disbelief, but I do recall sputtering about second opinions and specialists.

There were treatments, she clarified, possibly even more surgery, but no proven cure for her metastatic cancer.

"The doctor says I have about three years, on average," she added, her voice a dull monotone.

Tears came next, for both of us, along with incredulity. The metastasis was so small, surely it could be removed, eradicated; but, of course, life doesn't have cartoonish answers—a child's stick-figure drawing of surgery and doctors, a hospital room overflowing with flowers and boxes of chocolates, then a happily-ever-after ending with a big rainbow and sunshine.

While I rambled, clutching Kelly's hand, she straightened and swiped at her tears with a tissue.

"Can you tell I've been crying?" she asked.

"A little, but it doesn't matter. Let's head to your house. Everyone will understand," I said, along with a few other platitudes.

"We're still going to the fair." She checked her reflection in the vanity mirror and pulled a small bag of makeup out of her purse, fixing her face, hiding her anguish.

I didn't argue with her decision. Kelly's eldest daughter Shaelyn was showing her pig as part of the 4-H competition at the Western Idaho State Fair. Kelly would never disappoint one of her daughters.

They came first. Cancer would have to wait.

Dirt puffed under our feet as Kelly and I entered the 4-H pavilion. The August heat rippled in visible waves, and a water mirage formed on the asphalt road behind us. The odor of manure swirled everywhere.

On one side, a Jersey heifer blinked her brown eyes. Holsteins towered above us, their white patches gleaming, ready for the judges. We passed steers and goats with 4-H kids rushing around them, carrying buckets of water or hay.

My mind buzzed, worries almost erasing my surroundings; yet, Kelly floated ahead, outwardly serene. We clambered to the top of the bleachers, and the evening rolled on. Pig after pig, the judge imparting his porcine knowledge in small doses.

Soon Shaelyn entered the show area. Her hair wrapped around her shoulder in a thick braid, and her sea-green eyes were full of serious speculation. She moved with grace, unaware of her athletic ease, her pig following her lead, the culmination of a summer of practice.

Next came an older boy, tall and slender with a crewcut. His pigs followed his every movement, even a slight jerk of his head or twitch of a finger. And although Shaelyn, along with several other participants had looked exceptional, this boy, even to my inexperienced eye, was the clear winner.

Kelly knew him, having encountered him at other 4-H competitions, but we dubbed him, "The Pig Whisperer." After his performance, he joined us in the stands and chattered about his pigs, their feed, breeders in the Boise valley, and where he might go to college. Kelly listened, nodding and asking questions.

That night, Kelly celebrated the Pig Whisperer, a young man whom she barely knew, as he won award after award. She cheered him on because the air spun in a whirlpool of odors, both sweet and repugnant; yet speaking of animals and 4-H kids, reaffirming an endless cycle of life. She cheered because the sun glowed red in the sky, and the Idaho heat bore down on her.

On that day and almost every day after that, despite surgeries and treatment, she chose to cheer life's twists and turns. She celebrated and she grieved, but at no moment did she give up. Hope lived within her, cartwheeling and careening, refusing to accept defeat. She cheered because she breathed, because vitality coursed through her, because she knew no other way.

2. A TIMELESS LIFE

"Do you still want to swim laps?" my sister Kelly asked me as she eased behind the steering wheel of her early '90s Honda CRX.

Settling into the passenger seat, I laughed, positive she was joking. The dashboard clock read 6 p.m. The lap-swimming session had just begun, but the drive, in addition to parking and changing our clothes, would leave us about ten minutes to swim, at the most.

"I'm serious," she said. "I think we can make it."

And I believed her, knowing that she'd never accepted the 24-hour day. She'd convinced herself long ago that it had been replaced with 36 hours, allowing one to embrace each second, squeeze in another outing, or start a new project.

"No way," I said. "We don't have time."

"Are you sure?" She grinned, ready to race the clock, confident time would simply relent and mold to her needs.

Then would come the reward—a dive into an outdoor pool surrounded by palm trees. She would slice through the water, feeling the rush of bubbles with every flip turn, and catch a wedge of blue sky with each breath.

"Haven't we done enough today?" I grumbled, tired and slightly irritated.

On the back seat sat a pile of packages and shopping bags. Colorful Oaxacan wood carvings of angels and dragons mingled with hand-blown pitchers rimmed in dark blue, evidence of an afternoon spent wandering through Los Algodones, Mexico, a quick slip over the Arizona border.

In the morning, we had ridden Kelly's horses through the orange groves near her house as Stetson, her dog, scampered nearby. Next came a lunch of fish tacos and spicy ice-tea at our favorite restaurant.

The day had filled me up, taking all my energy. I needed a nap not laps.

Kelly dismissed my lack of enthusiasm with a shake of her head and reluctantly gave up on the pool. Instead, new plans were made. The evening stretched ahead of us with dinner, horse chores, and the promise of shadows dancing across the desert. We would sit on the porch and watch the sun slide across the horizon in splashes of red and orange, setting the desert on fire.

Over the years, "Do you still want to swim laps?" became my reminder to her that the hours in the day were finite. Sometimes she laughed at me; occasionally she seemed annoyed; but usually she ignored me.

The rest of the world could slog through their daily lives, accepting 24 hours. But not her. She wouldn't be content with such limitations.

I eventually stopped joking about time. She learned the lesson on her own, in a class taught by cancer.

But her instinct to live each day to its fullest never went away. It pushed her to fill every hour, despite radiation, surgeries, and chemotherapy. It brought her fulfillment and distinction—Idaho Nurse Practitioner of the Year and Idaho State University Distinguished Teacher.

She taught herself how to quilt and started a blog that linked quilting to her battle with cancer. She traveled to wrestling tournaments and swim meets with her youngest daughters and planned a high-school graduation party for her eldest. Lists were made; trips discussed.

Hope sat on her shoulder and sang in her ear. She never gave up, perhaps not even understanding that concept.

"Do you still want to swim laps?" she asked me almost 25 year ago.

And now I wished I'd said, "Hell, yes."

With the windows rolled down, soaking in the Arizona heat and our hair whipping around our faces, we would have zipped down the two-lane roads, leaving the dusty border town behind us. Squealing into the parking lot, only minutes left to swim, we would have jumped into the cool water and dashed out a few laps, for no other reason but to feel the sun on our bare arms and our hearts beat as we sprinted up and down the pool. Later, as we lay on the deck, we would have laughed about our crazy race across Yuma and our day packed full of memories.

Time was a theory to my sister, meant to be disproven. She lived as if each moment had significance, truly a gift to be savored. And she left behind a distinct beat, a clock of her own invention, available to all those who want to slip through life, dancing to their own rhythm.

3. READING IN TANDEM

"Hallie and I were so attached, like keenly mismatched Siamese twins conjoined at the back of the mind. We parted again and again and still each time it felt like a medical risk, as if we were being liberated at some terrible cost: the price of a shared organ. We never stopped feeling that knife."

I read that passage from Barbara Kingsolver's *Animal Dreams* during the summer of 1991, consuming the novel in almost one sitting. In the background, the window air conditioner of my one-bedroom apartment sputtered in a rhythmic ricochet like an expletive-laden rap, abusing me with its lack of cooling power.

A car backfired or a gun was shot—impossible to tell in my neighborhood—and I jumped. My flat, perched on top of restaurants and shops, Woody-Allenesque to my 20-something self, sat in a transitional zone, linking safety with seedy.

But the novel distracted me, and soon the outside world and heat of Stockton, California's Miracle Mile diminished. I curled up on the loveseat, glad to be safe in my cozy apartment, and allowed Kingsolver's soothing prose to refresh me.

"Hallie and I were so attached," I whispered, rereading the page.

The words soaked in, and I opened my heart to them. I explored their truth, something only the naivete of my years would have permitted, not having experienced the full range of loss and sorrow; disappointment and heartbreak.

Today, the passage would have been read once then set aside,

Kingsolver's description etched into my psyche, as if I'd slipped between the pages of the book. But in my 20s, a teenage sense of invincibility still clung to me. So I contemplated the quote, dwelling on separation and death, bringing myself to easily-dismissed tears.

Yes, bad things happened, I thought, but not to me or my family. Back then, the years stretched ahead in an endless tangle. My sister Kelly and I would ease into old age. I childishly imagined us as elderly ladies, living with our spouses in an enormous Victorian house, each having our own wing and meeting for meals and laughter and book-sharing.

I finished the novel, one of hundreds I've read over the years, and moved on to the next one. But it stayed with me, that quote, like a premonition.

Later, I passed *Animal Dreams* on to Kelly. It wasn't the first book we would share, a lifelong habit. Reading was automatic for us, as vital as air, but not every recommendation was read or ever discussed again.

Our literary tastes often diverged. As a teen, Kelly's first love was horror, a genre that had always repulsed me—the authors too successful at making the unbelievable come to life. As we matured, however, our interests intersected, often overlapping at the same time.

During the summer of 1988 we argued over our single copy of Scott Turow's *Presumed Innocent*, grumbling when one of us monopolized it for too long. We were working as lifeguards at a remote Alaskan outpost, so finding another copy was not simple. When we both reached the page-turning final chapters at the same time, we read aloud while watching the pool, usually devoid of swimmers.

Over the years, she steered me to *Mrs. Peregrine's School for Peculiar Children*, *The Guernsey Literary and Potato Peel Pie Society*, and *The Case for Christ*. Together, we cherished Elizabeth George mysteries, particularly the idiosyncratic Barbara Havers, cheering her successes.

One winter, after Kelly's cancer diagnosis, I read *Winter Solstice* by Rosamunde Pilcher. Snow fell outside in an endless tapestry, enveloping the house with a lacey shroud, erasing the rest of the world. Dusk blew a periwinkle tint onto the walls. Pilcher's story of loss and redemption spoke to me; her ability to find light in the most frightening circumstances filled me with hope.

I immediately passed it on to Kelly. Next came *The Shell Seekers*, and then, partially for myself, I purchased four of Pilcher's novels as a Christmas present for Kelly. But illness and treatments kept her from finishing them.

Those books are with me now, a reminder of life's twists and turns, at times cruel. Yet, Pilcher's words are a balm, acknowledging the pain of living while also finding a source for optimism, putting into words universal emotions that are difficult to explain, as Barbara Kingsolver did in *Animal Dreams*.

Kelly and I never discussed that novel, so I won't know if she also paused while reading, "We never stopped feeling that knife." But within the past several months, I've lived Kingsolver's words. The plunge of the knife made the final parting with my sister permanent.

Soon after the wound was made, I came across *Water for Elephants* at the bottom of a pile of books in Kelly's room. "That's my favorite novel," she once told me, reminding me from time to time, repeating herself, as we're all prone to do, particularly when reminiscing about good memories.

Kelly's copy of *Water for Elephants* sits on my bedside table. I will reread it often and imagine her skimming the words over my shoulder or reading aloud at the swimming pool.

Perhaps it will help the wound heal, stitched together by literature, but left behind will always be a scar, telling a story of loss mixed with Kelly's bravery and optimism. Maybe her tale will also be told to others, inspiring those who hear it to capture life, despite setbacks and disappointment.

Regardless, my braided scar with its twisted branches will forever retain the memory of a knife pricked by the wisdom of prose. It whispers to me of Barbara Kingsolver, sisterhood, and reading in tandem, a shared literary life.

4. THE WORLD STOPPED

"We're going to a marching band competition," I told Alan Kerrick, the funeral director, when he inquired about our plans for the day.

I prattled on, feeling like I had to explain why my family would attend such an event less than 24 hours before my sister Kelly's memorial service.

"Kelly's daughter is in the band," I said. "We're trying to keep the girls busy with their activities. A sense of normalcy."

"It's a distraction," I added, finally sputtering to an end.

"The world doesn't stop," Alan said. "Life must go on." He spoke calmly and in a soft tone, his manner a source of comfort during a difficult time, as I'm sure he had been—and continues to be—for countless families.

Alan had graduated from high school with Kelly, adding another layer to his compassion, a true sharing in my family's grief. He had even been in the drumline of the marching band, so he understood about the commitment to competitions.

Regardless, his words echoed in my psyche. How could the world keep spinning on its axis? Time continue slipping forward?

"The world should stop, if even just for a day," I said in that strange, honest, yet distant manner I acquired for a short time after Kelly's death.

I communicated through a surreal cloud, leaking words, raw emotions splattering around me, but my utterances didn't bring relief. The source, brimming with grief and anger, refilled in an instant.

Alan murmured something reassuring, accepting my unusual confession. His patience and kindness were genuine, and I thought about the sorrow he faced daily, how my reaction probably mirrored dozens of other mourners.

A part of me found solace in that thought—whether we live in the United States or Kazakhstan, our emotions run a universal spectrum. We all share in a common experience from our triumphs to our tragedies. To believe anything else is an exercise in egotism.

Despite all this, I meant what I had said. The world should have halted for one day with a collective wail, stretching across the continents and gathering strength, shaking the heavens.

Teeth gnashed.

Chests pounded.

Of course, none of this happened. Life tumbled forward with its bills to be paid, animals to be fed, appointments to be kept. On and on.

Which is exactly what Kelly would have wanted.

She celebrated life, its everyday messes and exhilarations, and although she might have wanted to harness time, cramming all her energy into every hour, she never would have asked anyone to put their existence on hold for a worldwide day of mourning. Her sense of selflessness wouldn't have allowed it.

So the earth keeps spinning, and maybe that in itself is a celebration of Kelly's life. Friends and family push forward, recognizing her final lessons of bravery and courage. We honor her most by following her bright example and continuing to engage in our everyday struggles.

The world might not have stopped, but her legacy continues to illuminate all who knew her and will reverberate through each us, reaching out to even those she never met.

5. GRACE NOTES

On October 10, 2016, thirteen helium balloons—carrying handwritten birthday greetings across their colorful surfaces—were released into a clear, Idaho sky.

Breezes tugged them across the pasture, where Indy, an elderly quarter horse, nodded his white head and swatted his tail, as if wanting to hurry them along, understanding their significance. They drifted, stretching across a wide horizon, their strings shimmying with the wind. Climbing higher, the balloons joined with clouds etched in pink and red, reflecting the setting sun.

The thirteen of us, family and friends, sang the Birthday Song, our voices at first faint but eventually gathering strength. Then we all stood there in silence, watching the floating greeting cards until they disappeared from sight.

And even though the intended recipient, my sister Kelly, was no longer with us, having left us only two days prior, I felt her presence, as I'm sure everyone did. Perhaps she was the feathery breeze brushing across our cheeks, the burst of wind chimes singing out into the dusky night, or the shadows darting around Indy.

Our simple gesture of remembrance had altered an evening ripe with anguish and sorrow into a night full of grace. And it was an eight-year-old girl, Lexie, who we had to thank for the transformative gift, a reflection of the love that my sister had generated throughout her life.

Quilting Cancer

Lexie had wanted to give Kelly a birthday present, telling her mother Mandy that she knew exactly how to deliver it, and Mandy made it possible, gathering all the supplies. Because of their initiative, it was easy to imagine the balloons, as they grew smaller, mere pinpricks against the vast sky, leaving this earth for a heavenly embrace.

It was one of many moments of grace over the past several years, during Kelly's long battle with cancer, in which generosity and selflessness fused together to defeat pain and fear, allowing us to transcend our grief and recognize how extraordinary and giving people can be.

These grace notes lived within Kelly and continue to envelop my family, filling our hearts with gratitude even as we mourn. And so this letter of thankfulness begins with a little girl, who understood that birthday celebrations never need to end, and continues with an almost endless list of people* who helped my sister carry her burden, trying to slip it off her shoulders, if only for a few seconds at a time…

Family

~ My nieces Shaelyn, Sierra, and Sheridan, whose maturity belies their years, filled Kelly with unwavering pride. They never faltered in their support and care for their mother, and their strength and character reflected off the people around them, making us all braver because of them.

~My mother Sherry and stepfather Pete wove a circle of love around Kelly and unconditionally supported her from traveling to Bethesda, MD to driving to doctor's appointments to simply holding her hand.

~My husband Keith offered endless optimism and humor—even when his heart was aching—without which our lives would have been much darker and bleaker places.

~Visits, calls, and cards from aunts, uncles, and cousins proved that the love of family stretches across any distance. Aunt Janean and cousins Ashley, Kendell, Jon, and Bella met Kelly and Sheridan at Washington swim meets. Uncle Jim, Aunt Kathy, Uncle John, and cousins Ian and Brad joined us at a Corvallis swim meet for a long weekend of sharing family memories. Cousin Liz and family visited

Kelly from Arizona, renewing their relationship and strengthening their love for each other. These visits meant so much to Kelly, and she often reflected on them, grateful to be a part of the Fanning-Walsh families.

St. Luke's MSTI

~Jonathon, Tonya, Karen, and all the nurses and staff never stopped fighting, despite the prognosis, and generated a sense of hope and courage through truthful optimism. Their compassion and kindness touched Kelly and my family and will continue to affect us for many years to come, perhaps forever, as I'm sure many families who have dealt with cancer can say. And, Patty, whose willingness to listen, always be available for guidance and comfort, has meant much more than I'm sure she realizes.

Friends from across the years and world

~Encouragement, love, and prayers arrived almost daily from friends across the world in the form of cards, online messages/texts, voice mails, visits, and flowers, often accompanied with a much-needed dose of humor. The names of these friends, from schools, organizations, and work, have run across my mind often over the past several years in a soothing litany: Sam, Beverly, Melody, Marilyn, Ben, Cristina, Bob, Xavier, Ann, Lanette, Rachel, Kristine, Pete, Gina, Lori, Tony, Kathy, Bruce, Carol, Peggy, Don, Hilary, Lucy, Susie, Rachael, Arlene, Roy... there are too many to name and some of whose actions were only known by Kelly. But please know that everything you did from lighting candles and donating to Aquathons to hospital visits brightened Kelly's journey during a very dark time and has had a lasting effect, engraved on the hearts of all who witnessed your deeds.

~And, of course, as in everyone's lives, there are friends who never quite fit into that category, who are more than that... Shane, Kelly's dear companion over the past few years and lifelong friend, became a partner in care, traveling to doctor's appointments across the United States and making himself available at all times (and continues to do so). And Twyla, more sister than friend, lifted Kelly with her humor and love.

Parma

~The support of the Parma community defies words. I'm at a loss to express how much this town and the people in it meant to Kelly. Cards arrived weekly from PEO sisters, and friends like Val, Jay, Kathy, Dana, Kristy, and many others frequently made themselves available to help or for a kind word. The teachers and staff of the Parma School District—Shelly, Toby, Madelyn, Monique, Patricia, Cory, Mick... everyone—wrapped my nieces in a supportive embrace and held them up during a difficult time. And Pastor Mark of Sterry Church spent hours and hours with Kelly, discussing Christ's message and guiding her on a spiritual path of hope and renewal.

Neighbors

~From weeding and snowplowing to providing dinners and taking care of animals or simply providing a hug, Kelly's neighbors—the Timmons, Jeffers, Parkers, Pascales, Mcleans, and Morrels—selflessly gave of their time. Mandy Pascale and her family offered tireless help, support, and friendship with Mandy recently completing three quilts that Kelly never had the chance to finish.

Kappa Kappa Gamma

~Thank you, Karena, for a friendship that transcends the meaning of that word and for teaching me that there is always time for the people we love, despite distance and schedules. And Nola, for walking next to Kelly (and me) over the past forty years from swim team to cross country and track to the University of Idaho, as well as all my Kappa sisters for your letters, messages, and visits over the past several years, along with the glorious anniversary weekend last April, which meant so much to Kelly and will be etched in my memory forever.

Swim Teams

~Boise YMCA Swim Team parents and swimmers became cheerleaders, not only for my nieces but also for Kelly. This outstanding organization provided much more than just an outlet for exercise and competition but grew into a much-loved activity and diversion, especially Coach Linda Conger, who texted Kelly daily with jokes and supplied us all with some of the best tamales in the Boise Valley.

~The reintroduction of a swim team in Parma began as Kelly's dream and will hopefully continue in the years to come as part of her legacy. All the swim team parents and swimmers were loving and supportive, but Coach Andres, in particular, became a dear friend, always in contact, whether visiting Kelly in the hospital or joining us for Thanksgiving and other family celebrations.

4-H

~Like the Boise Y Swim Team, 4-H took on a larger meaning through the leaders and members' support for Kelly and her daughters, particularly Mandy and Myrn, whose phone calls and cards continue today.

All these people and their love flowed through Kelly and continue to bolster us up as we navigate through our grief, extending peace like a river (to borrow from Isaiah 66:12). The kindness Kelly received and gave during her life will have a chain reaction, touching everyone who witnessed it, linking us together in an endless loop and making us more aware of other people in need. Which, in the end, would have been exactly what Kelly would have wanted.

Her life was, in a sense, one of service—nursing—tending to people in the broadest meaning of that word. She believed our purpose on earth was to help other people, and if that was the lesson she left, then I know she would have been proud.

And, as Lexie proved, Kelly continues to inspire, setting an example of bravery and optimism that pushes us all upward, beyond the edge of the horizon where magical balloons proclaim their love for a person whose birthday celebration extends forever.

*If I've forgotten someone, please forgive me but know that everything you did was remembered and greatly appreciated by Kelly.

6. RIDE IN PEACE

She lives now in an orange grove scented with an Arizona spring. Sand stretches in an endless transition from desert to brown velvet hills to jagged cliffs. Distant spires rip at clouds, creating a pathway from earth to heaven.

The sky extends across a limitless horizon, the blue of a tranquil sea, as if the world could be flipped upside down and a boat would appear. I imagine a ferry transporting her and her horse Indigo to unknown worlds.

But the sky stays in place, and she and Indy weave in and out of the groves, halting occasionally to allow Indy to bend his long neck and munch on fallen oranges. Her dog Stetson runs ahead, stopping at the rare puddle for a drink of muddy water.

The trees fall behind her, and with a touch of her heels, Indy springs ahead, galloping toward the towering mountains, where shadows gather and alpenglow hints at rose. Stetson trails, sprinting then lagging but never giving up.

She turns, ponytail bouncing, and stands up in her stirrups to wave in my direction. But she doesn't beckon, knowing I can't follow. In the distance, another rider waits on a craggy butte. He sits tall in his saddle, size 15 boots wedged into stirrups.

They vanish into the dusk, at ease with the gathering dark, an inner light guiding them on the trail. I'll see them again soon, in the orange-grove meditation, an intermediary place of memories and communion.

ABOUT THE AUTHORS

KELLY FANNING

(The following obituary was written by Sherry Fanning, Kelly's mother.)

Kelly Colleen Fanning

October 10, 1964 - October 8, 2016

The lamb will be their shepherd and God will wipe every tear from their eyes. *Revelation 7:17*

Our courageous, loving Kelly Colleen Fanning departed her Parma home October 8, 2016. Her final days, weeks, and months were spent enjoying the company of her family, numerous friends and most importantly, her three daughters, Shaelyn, Sierra, and Sheridan. Believing that life's challenges provided opportunity for leaving a legacy for her daughters, Kelly faced her 8-year battle with cancer with grace, dignity and courage. She also believed that the silver lining in her experience with cancer has been the amazing love and support that she received from family and friends. She described them as being her source of strength, courage, and hope. She acknowledged that if love could cure cancer she would be immune to the disease.

Kelly was born in Nampa, Idaho, October 10, 1964 to Sherry and Stan Fanning. She immediately began traveling with her parents as her father was experiencing his final year of professional football. Her early education was in Surrey County, England, Indianapolis, Indiana, and Mexico City, where she developed a lifelong interest in the Mexican culture and proficiency with the language. Kelly attended junior and senior high in Caldwell, Idaho, where she was senior class president and commencement speaker in 1982.

She attended the University of Idaho and was a member of Kappa Kappa Gamma. She graduated from the University of Mississippi with a degree in communicative disorders. Kelly also graduated from Arizona Western College with an associate degree in nursing, from Northern Arizona University with a bachelor's degree in nursing, a master's degree in family nurse practice (nurse practitioner) from Idaho State University, and a doctorate in Nursing Practices from the University of Alabama. She worked in home health care, hospital nursing in Nampa, and was a family nurse practitioner for over ten years in Wilder and Parma in the West Valley clinics.

In 2014 Kelly was named the Idaho Nurse Practitioner of the year and that same year she was awarded the Idaho State University Distinguished Teacher. In 2015 she was involved in obtaining a $1.5 million grant to assist Idaho State University's School of Nursing in providing health care for refugees.

In recent years Kelly was awarded a community award in Parma, Idaho. She was able to organize a summer swim team and was their coach for several years. Kelly was very involved with 4-H.

Kelly had so many interests. She had been a competitive swimmer, on the ski patrol in Alaska, a barrel racer in Arizona, and, when cancer slowed her down, she took up quilting.

Kelly was all about love. She was glad for the adventures she had and opportunities she had been given. She readily described her life as having been born to great parents who were also born to great parents, as having loved and been loved, and as blessed to travel through life with her sister, Erin, as her best friend. Kelly was so grateful for her many aunts, uncles, grandparents, cousins, her beloved brother-in-law Keith Radwanski, her dear companions and caregivers Shane Harris, P T Rathbone and his family. And she is also grateful for the fathers of her children Dan Starnes whom she married in 1986, and Doug Pesnell DVM, married in 2000, because without them she would not have her beloved children. Kelly considered motherhood to be the best of life's adventures and her three daughters her greatest source of joy. She reveled in their growing sense of independence and confidence and was proud of the young ladies they have become. She was impressed by their accomplishments, maturity beyond their years, and their resilient zest of life.

Kelly was baptized as an infant in Grace Episcopal Church in Nampa. She loved the Lord; she believed in Jesus Christ as her savior and life eternal. Kelly always looked for Christ in everybody.

Thank you Dr. Jonathan Swardloff, Patty Green, and the rest of the amazing staff at MSTI, Fruitland. Thank you also the Reverend Mark Cox of Sterry Memorial Church for traveling the journey with Kelly.

> "Though my soul may set in darkness, it will rise in perfect light. I have loved the stars too fondly to be fearful of the night."
> *Sarah Williams, Twilight Hours: A Legacy of Verse*

ERIN FANNING

Erin splits her time between the lakes and woods of northern Michigan and the mountains of central Idaho. She is an occasional writer and a constant reader, pulling herself away from books to hike, kayak, bike, snowshoe or ski with her husband Keith.

Made in the USA
Middletown, DE
09 February 2018